Comparing Minibeasts

Minibeast Senses

Charlotte Guillain

Heinemann
LIBRARY

www.heinemannlibrary.co.uk
Visit our website to find out more information about Heinemann Library books.

To order:

☎ Phone +44 (0) 1865 888066

▤ Fax +44 (0) 1865 314091

💻 Visit www.heinemannlibrary.co.uk

Heinemann Library is an imprint of Capstone Global Library Limited, a company incorporated in England and Wales having its registered office at 7 Pilgrim Street, London, EC4V 6LB – Registered company number: 6695582

Heinemann is a registered trademark of Pearson Education Limited, under licence to Capstone Global Library Limited

Text © Capstone Global Library Limited 2010
First published in hardback in 2010
The moral rights of the proprietor have been asserted.

Edited by Nancy Dickmann and Catherine Veitch
Designed by Joanna Hinton-Malivoire
Picture research by Elizabeth Alexander
Production by Duncan Gilbert and Victoria Fitzgerald
Originated by Heinemann Library
Printed and bound in China by South China Printing Company Ltd

ISBN 978 0 431 19491 2
14 13 12 11 10
10 9 8 7 6 5 4 3 2 1

British Library Cataloguing in Publication Data
Guillain, Charlotte.
Comparing minibeasts.
Senses.
573.8'712-dc22

Acknowledgements
We would would like to thank the following for permission to reproduce photographs: Getty Images p. **21** (DEA / CHRISTIAN RICCI); iStockphoto p. **17**; Photolibrary pp. **6** (Michael Dietrich/imagebroker.net), **9** (David M Dennis/OSF), **7** (OSF), **14** (Jack Clark/Animals Animals), **15** (Klaus Honal/ age footstock), **16** (Herbert Zettl/Cusp), **23 middle** (Jack Clark/Animals Animals), **23 bottom** (Klaus Honal/age footstock); Shutterstock pp. **4** (© Cathy Keifer), **5** (© Anton Chernenko), **18** (© Hway Kiong Lim), **8** (© Kirsanov), **10** (© Tompi), **11** (© Sascha Burkard), **12** (© Neale Cousland), **13** (© Danijel Micka), **19** (© Armin Rose), **20** (© orionmystery@flickr), **22 top left** (© Studio Araminta), **22 bottom left** (© RCL), **22 middle top** (© Vinicius Tupinamba), **22 right** (© Ivelin Radkov), **23 top** (© Neale Cousland).

Cover photograph of a jumping spider reproduced with permission of FLPA (Mark Moffett/Minden Pictures). Back cover photograph of a night butterfly (Actias artemis) reproduced with permission of Shutterstock (© Kirsanov).

The publishers would like to thank Nancy Harris and Kate Wilson for their assistance in the preparation of this book.

Every effort has been made to contact copyright holders of material reproduced in this book. Any omissions will be rectified in subsequent printings if notice is given to the publishers.

Contents

Meet the minibeasts 4

Smell and taste 6

Feeling .12

Hearing .16

Seeing .18

How big? 22

Picture glossary 23

Index 24

Meet the minibeasts

There are many different types
of minibeasts.

Minibeasts can smell and taste.

They can also feel, hear, and see.

Smell and taste

Minibeasts smell and taste in different ways.

antennae

Insects use their antennae to smell and taste.

antennae

A moth uses its antennae to smell other minibeasts.

hairs

A spider uses hairs on its legs to smell other minibeasts.

tongue

Some insects use their tongues to taste food.

feet

Some insects use their feet to taste food.

Feeling

antennae

Minibeasts feel in different ways.
Many minibeasts feel with their
antennae.

hairs

Many minibeasts feel with hairs on their bodies.

tail

Some minibeasts feel things moving with their tails.

web

Spiders can feel things moving on their webs.

Hearing

Minibeasts hear in different ways.
A grasshopper can use its body to
hear things.

A praying mantis can use its body to hear things.

Seeing

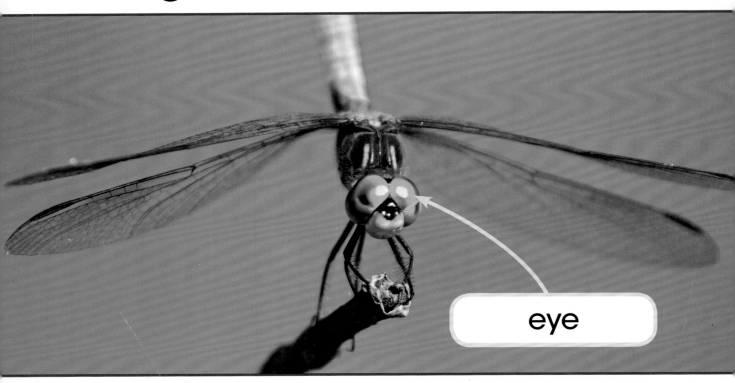

eye

Minibeasts see in different ways.

Insects have special eyes.

little eyes

Insect eyes are made of many
little eyes. Each little eye sees
something different.

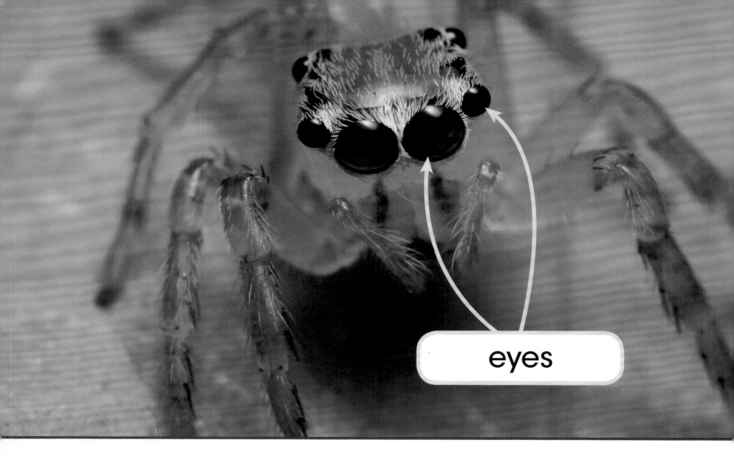

eyes

Spiders have six or eight eyes.

Earthworms do not have eyes.

How big?

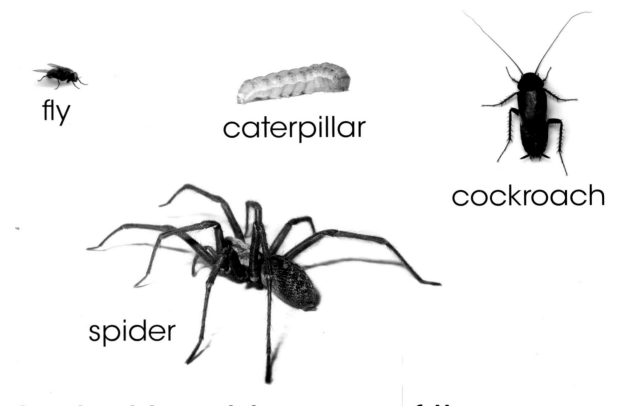

fly

caterpillar

cockroach

spider

Look at how big some of the minibeasts in this book can be.

Picture glossary

 **antenna** long, thin feeler on the head of an insect

 **insect** very small creature with six legs

 **web** net that spiders make to catch insects

Index

feel 5, 12, 13, 14, 15

hear 5, 16, 17

see 5, 18, 19

smell 5, 6, 7, 8, 9

taste 5, 6, 7, 10, 11

Notes to parents and teachers

Before reading

Make a list of minibeasts with the children. Try to include insects, arachnids (e.g. spiders), crustaceans (e.g. woodlice), myriapods (e.g. centipedes and millipedes), earthworms, slugs, and snails. Ask them if they know what our five senses are. Do they think minibeasts have the same senses as us? Do they have eyes, ears, noses, or tongues like us?

After reading

• Make minibeast masks showing eyes and antennae. Ask the children to choose a minibeast, such as a spider, moth, bee, or dragonfly. Look carefully at pictures of their chosen minibeasts and discuss the colour and number of their eyes. Are they made up of many small eyes? If they have antennae, what are they like? Use card, shiny paper and wrappers, tissue paper, and pipe cleaners to make masks of minibeast faces.

• Between spring and late summer you could go out of the classroom looking for flowers. Which flowers are bees and butterflies visiting? Ask the children to smell and observe the colour of these flowers. What do they notice? Help the children to draw up tally charts to record how many flying insects visit each coloured flower. Is there a colour preference?